THE
EMOTIONAL INTIMACY
BLUEPRINT

Your Guide to A Deeper, Lasting Connection

Copyright 2024: Happy Couples Connect

INDEX

Introduction: **Fostering Connection Through Effective Communication**

Chapter 1: **The Importance of Emotional Connection/Intimacy**

Chapter 2: **Understanding the Disconnect**

Chapter 3: **The Power of Regular Check-Ins**

Chapter 4: **The Vital Role of Conflict Resolution in Emotional Connection**

Chapter 5: **Let's Reconnect – Exercises**

Final Thoughts: **A Journey, Not a Destination**

INTRODUCTION

Have you ever looked across the dinner table and felt like you were miles apart, even though you're sitting right next to each other?

That feeling of disconnection can creep into any relationship, leaving you feeling lonely and unheard. But the good news is, that a strong emotional connection is absolutely achievable, and it's the key to a truly fulfilling partnership.

In this guide, we'll explore the power of emotional connection and why it matters so much. We'll also delve into some common reasons couples might feel disconnected like the ones therapist Gary Chapman explores in his book The 5 Love Languages.

We'll learn how our unique ways of giving and receiving love can sometimes lead to misunderstandings, and what we can do to bridge that gap

Most importantly, we'll equip you with practical tools and exercises to help you reconnect with your partner and build a stronger bond than ever before.

INTRODUCTION

This journey isn't about grand gestures or expensive dates; it's about the small, everyday moments of connection that create a lifetime of love and understanding.

Now, before we proceed, you need to know this:

True growth is self-motivated. If you're changing your part of the relationship issues just to get your partner to change too, you are setting yourself up for disappointment.

You want your partner to grow with you so you can feel closer, I get it. But, basing your own growth on whether you get the desired response, is a part of the problem, not the solution.

Grow for yourself first! Become the person you want to be. This will contribute to a healthier environment in the relationship and increase the odds of your partner catching on. True growth is about the long-game, not a quick fix.

Let's dive in.

CHAPTER 1

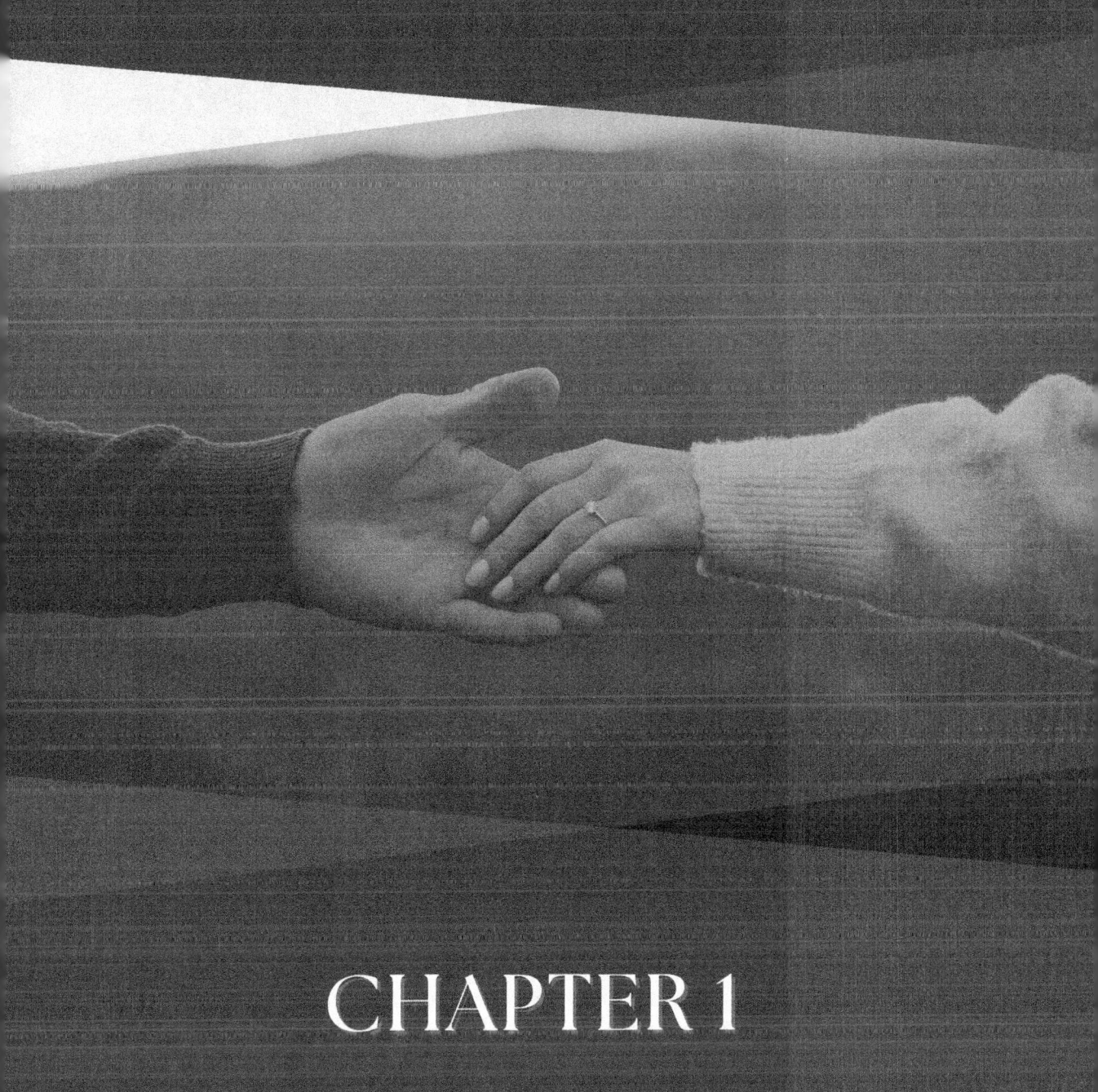

Intimacy is not purely physical. It's the act of connecting with someone so deeply, you feel like you can see into their soul."

- Unknown -

CHAPTER 1

WHAT IS EMOTIONAL CONNECTION?

Imagine this: you and your partner are facing a tough challenge together. Maybe it's a job search, a family issue, or just the daily grind. You feel completely understood and supported by them.

You can share your worries and fears without judgment, and you know they'll be there for you, no matter what. That's the power of emotional connection.

Emotional connection, or intimacy, is that deep sense of closeness and understanding you share with your partner. It's feeling safe enough to be vulnerable, knowing they'll truly "get" you.

It's about trust, empathy, and a shared sense of security. It's different from physical intimacy, although they can definitely go hand-in-hand.

Think about it like this: physical intimacy is the spark, but emotional connection is the fuel that keeps the fire burning bright in a relationship.

CHAPTER 1

WHY IS EMOTIONAL CONNECTION IMPORTANT?

So why is this emotional connection so important? Here's the thing: strong emotional connection is the foundation of a happy and healthy relationship.

It brings you closer, creates a sense of security, and allows you to weather life's storms together. Here are some of the amazing benefits of feeling connected to your partner:

- Stronger Support System: You know you can rely on each other for anything, big or small.
- Deeper Happiness: Sharing your joys and triumphs with someone who truly celebrates them with you creates a deeper sense of happiness.
- Better Communication: You feel comfortable expressing your needs and feelings openly and honestly.
- Conflict Resolution: You can navigate disagreements more effectively because you have a strong foundation of trust and understanding.

CHAPTER 1

On the other hand, a lack of emotional connection can leave you feeling lonely, isolated, and misunderstood in your relationship. It can lead to:

- Increased Conflict: Feeling unheard and unsupported can easily escalate arguments.
- Resentment: Bottling up your feelings can lead to bitterness over time.
- Loneliness: Even when you're physically together, you can feel emotionally distant.

The good news? No matter where you are on the connection spectrum, there are always ways to improve and build a stronger bond with your partner. Let's explore some signs that you feel disconnected in the next section.

ARE YOU FEELING DISCONNECTED?

Imagine you and your partner are driving down a highway. You started the trip together, excited for the destination. But somewhere along the way, you got distracted, maybe by phones, work, or just the daily hustle.

CHAPTER 1

Now, you realize you're in different lanes, drifting further apart. That's what can happen in relationships too.

Here are some signs that you and your partner might be feeling emotionally disconnected:

- Silence and Distance: Conversations feel forced or nonexistent. You spend more time on your phones or with other distractions than with each other.
- Feeling Unheard: You share your thoughts and feelings, but you don't feel truly listened to or understood.
- Increased Conflict: Arguments erupt easily, and you have trouble resolving them constructively.
- Emotional Withdrawal: You shut down emotionally, withdrawing from intimacy or affection.

These signs don't necessarily mean your relationship is doomed! They're simply signals that it's time to hit the brakes, reconnect, and get back on track together.

SELF-ASSESSMENT: QUESTIONS

CHAPTER 1

To help you identify areas for improvement, take a moment to reflect on these questions individually and then discuss them with your partner.

- How often do you have meaningful conversations about your day, hopes, and dreams?
- Do you feel comfortable expressing your vulnerabilities and emotions to your partner?
- Do you celebrate each other's successes and offer support during challenges?
- After an argument, do you repair the situation, or do you stay distant?

By being honest with yourself and your partner, you can start to understand the root causes of your disconnection and begin the journey back to a stronger bond.

WHY YOU ARE FEELING DISCONNECTED?

Here are some common reasons why couples might feel disconnected:

CHAPTER 1

- **Lack of Quality Time:** Busy schedules, distractions like technology, and falling into routines can leave little room for meaningful connection.
- **Communication Breakdown:** Not expressing needs clearly, interrupting, or avoiding difficult conversations can lead to misunderstandings and resentment.
- **Neglecting Love Languages:** If you're speaking different "love languages" and not showing love in ways your partner appreciates, they might feel unloved or unimportant.
- **Unresolved Conflict:** Holding onto anger or resentment from past arguments can create emotional distance.
- **Life Changes and Stress:** Major life events like job changes, moving, or having children can put a strain on your relationship and make it harder to connect.
- **Differing Attachment Styles:** If you have different attachment styles (secure, anxious, avoidant), it can affect how comfortable you feel with intimacy and vulnerability.
- **External Influences:** Stress from work, family issues, or financial problems can take a toll on your emotional bandwidth and make it harder to connect with your partner.

CHAPTER 1

By understanding these potential causes, you can identify areas for improvement and start rebuilding a stronger emotional connection.

DIFFERENT WAYS TO RECONNECT WITH YOUR PARTNER

Remember that feeling of falling head over heels for your partner? The good news is, that spark doesn't have to fade away over time. Reconnecting with your partner and keeping that flame alive is absolutely achievable. Here are some diverse ways to reignite the spark in your relationship: Here are some ideas to help you reconnect with your partner beyond just conversation:

Shared Activities and Experiences:

- **Revisit Your Passions:** Did you bond over a shared love for hiking or cooking classes? Rekindle that spark by revisiting those activities you both enjoyed early in the relationship.

CHAPTER 1

- **Explore New Adventures:** Step outside your comfort zone and try something new together. Take a dance class, go rock climbing, or learn a new language as a couple.
- **Volunteer Together:** Giving back to the community can be a powerful bonding experience. Find a cause you both care about and volunteer your time together.
- **Plan a Getaway:** Even a short weekend trip can break the routine and create space for focused connection. Escape to a cozy cabin, explore a new city, or simply relax on a beach getaway.

Small Gestures of Love:

- **Love Notes and Reminders:** Leave a sweet note hidden in their lunchbox or write a heartfelt message on the bathroom mirror.
- **Acts of Service:** Take a chore off their plate they usually dread, like running errands or doing the dishes.
- **Thoughtful Gifts:** It doesn't have to be expensive! A small bouquet of their favorite flowers or their favorite candy bar shows you're thinking of them.

CHAPTER 1

- **Random Acts of Affection:** A surprise hug, a lingering kiss, or a back rub can go a long way in expressing your love and appreciation.

Quality Time Together:

- **Unplug and Reconnect:** Put away your phones and laptops for a designated "free" evening. Focus on being present and engaged with each other.
- **Plan a Date Night (Even at Home!):** Recreate the spark of those early dates with a special dinner at home, complete with candles and conversation.
- **Cuddle Up and Watch a Movie:** Sometimes, the simplest things can be the most meaningful. Snuggle on the couch and enjoy a movie or show you both love.
- **Engage in Shared Hobbies:** Do you both enjoy reading? Spend some time curled up with a good book and discuss it afterward. If you love board games, have a fun game night at home.

CHAPTER 1

Remember:

- The key is to find activities and gestures that resonate with your unique relationship and love languages.

- Consistency is key! Small, regular efforts towards connection are more impactful than grand gestures once in a blue moon.

- Most importantly, have fun and enjoy each other's company!

NOTES

NOTES

NOTES

CHAPTER 2

"It's easy to feel uncared for when people aren't able to communicate and connect with you in the way you need."

– Unknown –

CHAPTER 2

THE ROLE OF LOVE LANGUAGES IN EMOTIONAL CONNECTION

Have you ever felt like you're speaking different languages in your relationship? You put in all this effort to show you care, but your partner just doesn't seem to get it. Well, there might be a simple explanation: you might be speaking different "love languages".

This concept comes from therapist Gary Chapman's book The 5 Love Languages. According to Chapman, we all have preferred ways of giving and receiving love.

Just like some people prefer learning visually, others might learn best through hearing. Similarly, some people feel most loved through acts of service, while others crave words of affirmation.

Here's a quick overview of the 5 Love Languages:

1. Words of Affirmation: These folks thrive on compliments, words of encouragement, and expressions of appreciation.

CHAPTER 2

2. Acts of Service: Actions speak louder than words for this group. Doing chores, running errands, or anything that makes their life easier shows you care.

3. Receiving Gifts: It's not about materialism! For these individuals, a thoughtful gift, no matter how big or small, is a symbol of your love and attention.

4. Quality Time: This group craves focused, uninterrupted time with you. Put away the distractions and simply connect on a deeper level.

5. Physical Touch: Holding hands, cuddling, or any form of physical affection is a major way these individuals feel loved and secure.

THE ROLE OF ATTACHMENT STYLES IN EMOTIONAL CONNECTION

Another factor that can influence emotional connection is our attachment style. This is a concept developed in psychology that explains how early childhood experiences shape our relationships. There are three main attachment styles:

CHAPTER 2

1. Secure Attachment: People with this style feel comfortable with intimacy and trust their partners to be there for them.

2. Anxious Attachment: These individuals often crave reassurance and might worry about their partner's commitment.

3. Avoidant Attachment: People with this style tend to be uncomfortable with closeness and might push partners away.

Understanding your attachment style and your partner's can help you navigate communication challenges and build a more secure bond.

THE ROLE OF COMMUNICATION STYLES IN EMOTIONAL CONNECTION

Have you ever felt like you and your partner are speaking different languages? Communication styles play a significant role in how we connect with others.

CHAPTER 2

Some people are naturally direct and assertive, while others are more indirect or avoidant. Here are some common communication styles:

- **Passive:** People with this style tend to bottle up their emotions and avoid expressing their needs. This can lead to resentment and frustration in the relationship.
- **Aggressive:** Individuals with this style often express their emotions in a way that is hurtful or disrespectful. This can create tension and distance in the connection.
- **Assertive:** This is the ideal communication style for healthy relationships. Assertive communicators express their needs clearly and directly, while also respecting the feelings of others.

The problem? There's no single "right" communication style. What works for you might not work for your partner. Here's where emotional intelligence comes in.

THE ROLE OF COMMUNICATION STYLES IN EMOTIONAL CONNECTION

CHAPTER 2

- **Active Listening:** A cornerstone of EQ, active listening involves truly paying attention to your partner, both verbally and nonverbally. This means putting away distractions, making eye contact, and asking clarifying questions to ensure you understand their perspective.
- **Empathy:** Seeing things from your partner's point of view and acknowledging their feelings is crucial for building connection.
- **Assertive Communication:** Express your needs and feelings honestly and directly, but without being aggressive or accusatory.

By developing these EQ skills, you can adapt your communication style to better suit your partner's needs. This creates a safe space for open communication, fostering a deeper emotional connection in your relationship.

Wait... What is Emotional Intelligence?

Imagine you're having a disagreement with your partner. Your emotions flare up – maybe you feel frustrated or angry. But instead of lashing out, you take a deep breath
and try to understand why you're feeling that way.

CHAPTER 2

You then express your needs calmly and listen attentively to your partner's perspective. This ability to manage your emotions and navigate relationships effectively is what emotional intelligence (EQ) is all about.

EQ is more than just being "good" with your emotions. It's a complex set of skills that allows you to:

- **Understand your emotions:** Recognize your feelings as they arise and identify the situations or triggers that cause them.
- **Manage your emotions:** Instead of letting emotions control you, you can regulate them in a healthy way. This might involve taking a time-out, using relaxation techniques, or expressing your feelings constructively.
- **Motivate yourself:** EQ helps you set goals, stay focused, and persevere through challenges.
- **Empathize with others:** You can understand and share the feelings of others, fostering stronger connections.
- **Build and maintain relationships:** EQ allows you to communicate effectively, resolve conflict constructively, and create a sense of trust and intimacy.

CHAPTER 2

WHY IS EQ IMPORTANT FOR CONNECTION?

Think of emotional intelligence as the foundation for a strong relationship. Here's why it matters so much:

- **Stronger Self-Awareness:** When you understand your own emotions, you can communicate your needs clearly and avoid unintentionally hurting your partner.
- **Deeper Empathy:** By recognizing and understanding your partner's emotions, you can be more supportive and nurturing in the relationship.
- **Effective Communication:** EQ skills like active listening and assertive communication help you express yourself clearly and listen attentively to your partner, fostering a deeper connection.
- **Conflict Resolution:** When emotions run high, EQ allows you to manage the situation calmly, navigate disagreements constructively, and find solutions that work for both of you.

CHAPTER 2

Building emotional intelligence is a journey, not a destination. But by making a conscious effort to understand and manage your emotions, you can create a more fulfilling and connected relationship with your partner.

THE ROLE OF VULNERABILITY AND TRUST IN EMOTIONAL CONNECTION

Imagine a relationship as a garden. Sure, you need sunshine and water for it to flourish, but what truly allows deep roots to grow? Vulnerability and trust.

Vulnerability:

This is the willingness to open yourself up emotionally, sharing your fears, dreams, and insecurities with your partner. It's about letting your guard down and allowing them to see you, truly you.

CHAPTER 2

- Justifying the behavior or words instead of apologizing
- Choosing not to listen to your partner's perspective
- Getting angry and verbally attacking
- Putting the blame back on your partner
- Not willing to compromise or resolve
- Playing the victim
- Making excuses about the concerns that are brought up
- Minimizing the partner's feelings or concerns
- Interrupting or talking over the partner
- Reacting with sarcasm or contempt
- Avoiding responsibility by shifting focus to unrelated issues

THE IMPACT OF DEFENSIVENESS ON COMMUNICATION

Defensiveness is like a wall that we erect between ourselves and our partners, preventing authentic connection and understanding.

When we become defensive, we're more focused on protecting our ego than on truly listening to and empathizing with our partner's perspective.

CHAPTER 2

Note: Vulnerability isn't a sign of weakness, it's a testament to your strength and courage. It takes real bravery to open up, to show your true self, especially when there's a chance of being hurt. But by being vulnerable, you're allowing yourself to be seen, understood, and connected with on a deeper level.

While vulnerability can feel scary, it's essential for building intimacy. Here's why:

- **Deeper Connection:** Sharing your vulnerabilities allows your partner to connect with you on a deeper level, fostering a sense of closeness and understanding.
- **Trust Building:** When you open yourself up, it shows your partner that you trust them with your heart. This trust is essential for a secure and lasting relationship.
- **Emotional Intimacy:** Vulnerability creates a safe space for intimacy to blossom. You can truly be yourself around your partner, without fear of judgment.

CHAPTER 2

Trust:

The foundation of any strong relationship, trust is built through consistent positive actions. It involves:

- **Honesty:** Being truthful and reliable, even when it's difficult.
- **Respect:** Valuing your partner's feelings and needs.
- **Fidelity:** Remaining loyal and committed to your partner.
- **Accountability:** Taking responsibility for your actions and words.

By nurturing both vulnerability and trust, you create a safe space for emotional connection to thrive in your relationship.

IDENTIFY YOUR PATTERNS

Now that you've learned about love languages, attachment styles, communication styles and emotional intellegence, it's time to do some detective work!

CHAPTER 2

Here are some links to resources that can help you and your partner identify your unique patterns. Simply type the link into your internet browser.

- Love Language Quiz - https://shorturl.at/w3Wxb

- Attachment Style Quiz - https://shorturl.at/rO5BE

- Communication Style Quiz - https://shorturl.at/OGMkg

- EQ Quiz - https://shorturl.at/eOdsS

Once you've established your love language, attachment style, communication style and emotional intelligence level, discuss the results with your partner.

By understanding your individual needs and communication styles, you can start to bridge the gap and build a stronger emotional connection.

NOTES

NOTES

NOTES

CHAPTER 3

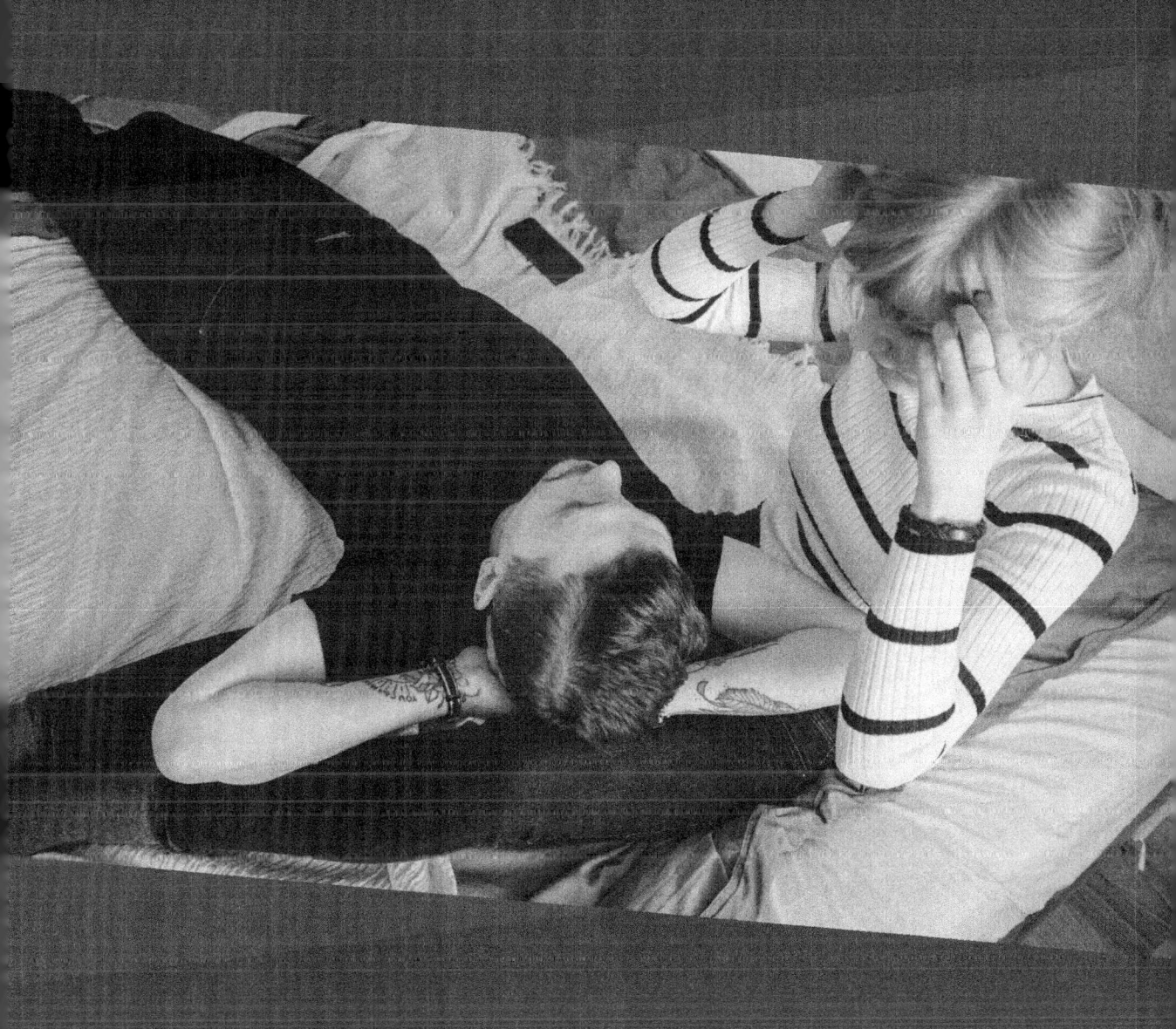

""The best relationships are built on a foundation of trust, which is nurtured through regular check-ins and open communication."

- Unknown -

CHAPTER 3

WHY WEEKLY CHECK-INS MATTER

Imagine your relationship as a garden. To keep it flourishing, you need to tend to it regularly, right? Weekly check-ins are like fertilizer for your emotional connection.

They provide a dedicated space to nurture your bond, address any concerns, and simply reconnect with your partner.

Here's why regular check-ins are so important:

- **Strengthen Communication:** Check-ins create a safe space for open and honest communication, which is the foundation of any strong relationship.
- **Preventative Maintenance:** Addressing small issues before they become bigger problems can prevent unnecessary conflict and frustration.
- **Deeper Connection:** Regular check-ins show your partner that you value their thoughts, feelings, and well-being. It fosters a sense of shared journey and strengthens the emotional bond.
- **Quality Time:** Check-ins ensure you dedicate uninterrupted time to connect with your partner, away from distractions and daily routines.

CHAPTER 3

SETTING THE STAGE

Now that you're convinced about the power of check-ins, let's talk about setting the stage for success. Here are some tips to create a positive and productive atmosphere:

- **Schedule Time:** Choose a specific day and time each week that works for both of you. Stick to the schedule as much as possible to avoid feeling rushed or stressed.
- **Find a Quiet Space:** Put away distractions like phones and laptops. Choose a comfortable and private space where you can focus on each other.
- **Set Ground Rules:** Agree on some basic communication guidelines, like active listening and avoiding interrupting. This ensures a safe space for open and honest expression.

THE CHECK-IN CONVERSATION

Here's a basic structure to guide your check-in conversations:

1. Appreciations: Start by expressing gratitude for your partner. Did they do something thoughtful? Mention it!

CHAPTER 3

2. Positives: Share the highlights of your week. What are you happy about? What are you looking forward to?
3. Challenges: Discuss any challenges you're facing, personally or as a couple. Be open and honest about your feelings.
4. Needs: Let your partner know how they can best support you this week. What do you need most from them?
5. Goals: Discuss any shared goals you have as a couple, big or small.

Bonus Tip: End your check-in on a positive note! Perhaps cuddle on the couch, share a laugh, or simply express your love for each other.

EXPLORING FEELINGS

Honest and open communication is the cornerstone of any strong relationship. But simply talking isn't enough. To truly connect on an emotional level, you need to create a safe space where both partners feel comfortable expressing their feelings freely. Here's how:

CHAPTER 3

- **Active Listening:** This goes beyond simply hearing the words your partner says. Pay close attention to their nonverbal cues like body language and tone of voice. Show them you're engaged by making eye contact, nodding, and summarizing what you've heard.
- **Empathy:** Try to see things from your partner's perspective and acknowledge their feelings, even if you don't necessarily agree. Phrases like "I understand why you feel that way" or "It sounds like you're feeling frustrated" can go a long way.
- **Non-judgmental Environment:** Let your partner know that they can express themselves openly and honestly without fear of criticism or judgment.
- **Respectful Communication:** Avoid interrupting or talking over your partner. Use "I" statements to express your needs and feelings, such as "I feel hurt when..." instead of accusatory statements like "You always..."
- **Focus on Understanding:** The goal of check-in conversations isn't to "win" or place blame. It's about understanding each other's perspectives and working together to find solutions.

By creating this safe and supportive environment, you encourage your partner to open up emotionally, fostering a deeper connection.

CHAPTER 3

IDENTIFYING AND ARTICULATING YOUR FEELINGS

Sometimes, simply saying "I feel bad" isn't enough. Being able to identify and articulate your emotions more precisely can lead to more productive and meaningful conversations. Here are some tips:

- Expand Your Emotional Vocabulary: Move beyond basic emotions like happy, sad, or angry. Explore a wider range of feelings like frustrated, disappointed, content, or hopeful.
- **Consider the Context:** Think about what triggered your emotions. What situation or event led you to feel this way? Understanding the context can help you communicate your feelings more effectively.
- **Use "I" Statements:** Express how your partner's actions or words made you feel. For example, "I felt hurt when you said…" is more constructive than simply saying "You hurt me".
- **Nonverbal Cues:** While words are important, nonverbal communication plays a role too. Maintain eye contact, use appropriate facial expressions, and avoid crossing your arms, which can appear defensive.

CHAPTER 3

Bonus Tip: If you struggle to identify your emotions, consider keeping a journal. Take some time each day to reflect on your experiences and write down how you're feeling. This can help you gain greater awareness of your emotional landscape.

By following these tips, you can create a safe space for emotional connection in your relationship and have more meaningful conversations about your feelings. Remember, open and honest communication is essential for building a strong emotional connection with your partner.

QUESTIONS TO ASK YOUR PARTNER

Here are some questions you can ask your partner to reconnect, categorized to target different aspects of your relationship:

General Connection and Appreciation:

- What's one thing that made you smile this week?

- What's something you're proud of that you accomplished recently?

CHAPTER 3

- What's a quality you really appreciate about me?

- Is there anything I can do to support you more this week?

- Looking back on our relationship, what's a favorite memory you cherish?

Deeper Emotional Connection:

- If you could describe our relationship in three words, what would they be?

- Is there anything you've been wanting to talk about but haven't felt comfortable bringing up?

- What are you most looking forward to in our future together?

- When was a time you felt most loved by me?

Is there a dream you have that you haven't shared with me yet?

CHAPTER 3

Understanding Each Other Better:

- What does a perfect day look like to you?

- If you could change one thing about yourself, what would it be?

- What are your biggest fears or anxieties right now?

- What are some things you're passionate about that I might not know about?

- What is your love language (refer back to Chapter 2)? How can I show you I care in a way that truly resonates with you?

Strengthening Communication:

- Is there anything I do that unintentionally hurts your feelings?

Do you feel like I listen to you fully and understand your point of view?

CHAPTER 3

- Is there a way I can communicate my needs to you more effectively?

- What are some things I can do to be more supportive during a disagreement?

How can we feel more comfortable expressing our vulnerabilities to each other?

MORE QUESTIONS TO ASK EACH OTHER TO DEEPEN YOUR EMOTIONAL CONNECTION.

- What is one thing that I do that always makes you feel loved and appreciated?

- What do you envision our ideal home life looking and feeling like?

- How do you think we've both changed individually since we first met, and how has that affected our relationship?

- How can we better navigate differences in opinions or values?

CHAPTER 3

- What activities or rituals make you feel closest to me?

- Are there unresolved issues or concerns you'd like to address?

- Are there topics or conversations you feel hesitant to bring up with me?

- What aspects of our relationship do you consider non-negotiable?

- How do you define emotional intimacy, and how can we deepen it?

- What kind of support do you need when going through tough times?

Remember:

- The most important thing is to ask these questions with genuine curiosity and a desire to connect with your partner.

CHAPTER 3

- Actively listen to their responses and avoid interrupting.

- Be open to hearing things that might be difficult, and respond with empathy and understanding.

EXPRESSING GRATITUDE:

Taking the time to express gratitude is a powerful way to strengthen your emotional connection. Here are some prompts and examples to get you started:

- **Specific Appreciation:** "I really appreciate you taking care of the groceries this week. It took a lot off my plate."
- **Effort Recognition:** "I know you don't always enjoy cooking, but that dinner you made last night was delicious. Thank you for putting in the effort."
- **Positive Traits:** "I feel so lucky to have someone as supportive and understanding as you in my life."
- **Simple Gestures:** "Thank you for always making the coffee in the morning. It's a small thing, but it means a lot to me."
- **Open Ended Prompt:** "Thinking about the week, what's one thing I did that made you feel appreciated or cared for?"

CHAPTER 3

HOLDING YOUR PARTNER ACCOUNTABLE

Accountability isn't just a relationship buzzword; it's a superpower that strengthens your emotional connection with your partner in profound ways.

Here's how taking responsibility and holding each other accountable fosters a deeper and more fulfilling bond:

- **Trust Building:** Accountability is the bedrock of trust. When partners consistently follow through on commitments and hold themselves accountable for their actions, it builds confidence and security. You know you can rely on each other, creating a safe space for vulnerability and emotional intimacy to blossom.

- **Communication and Understanding:** Holding each other accountable requires open and honest communication. Discussing expectations, boundaries, and goals fosters a deeper understanding of each other's needs and values. This transparency builds empathy, compassion, and a sense of being truly heard – all essential ingredients for a strong emotional connection.

CHAPTER 3

- **Respect and Validation:** Accountability goes hand-in-hand with respect. It's about acknowledging your partner's feelings, perspectives, and individuality. When you hold each other accountable with empathy and respect, it validates their emotions and experiences within the relationship. Feeling valued and understood strengthens the emotional connection by affirming your partner's worth.

- **Mutual Support and Growth:** Accountability is about supporting each other's journey, both individually and as a couple. Encouraging and challenging each other to honor commitments, pursue goals, and work on areas for improvement demonstrates a genuine investment in each other's well-being and success. This mutual support fosters a sense of teamwork and shared purpose, deepening your emotional connection.

- **Conflict Resolution and Repair:** Accountability is a game-changer in navigating conflict. When disagreements arise, partners who take responsibility for their contributions and work together towards solutions build resilience and trust. This proactive approach to conflict resolution allows you to repair and strengthen your emotional connection, emerging from challenges even stronger.

CHAPTER 3

- **Shared Responsibility and Intimacy:** Accountability reinforces the idea of shared responsibility within a relationship. Holding yourselves accountable for upholding agreements, meeting each other's needs, and nurturing the relationship creates a sense of partnership and intimacy. You're not just two individuals; you're a team facing life's challenges together, knowing you can rely on each other for support and understanding. This shared responsibility fosters a deeper emotional connection.

HOLDING EACH OTHER ACCOUNTABLE LOOKS LIKE:

"I'm feeling a little stressed about …. And I took it out on you. I'm sorry, you didn't deserve that."

"I got defensive earlier and said some hurtful things. I'm sorry! Can we try to talk again so I can listen better?"

"I didn't communicate my needs. I expected you to know. I'm sorry, I will work on being more clear."

"I owe you an apology for being passive-aggressive earlier. I'm sorry! I will be more mindful of my tone."

CHAPTER 3

By embracing accountability, you cultivate a relationship rich in trust, communication, respect, and mutual support. Remember, it's not about punishment; it's about creating a safe space for growth and fostering an emotional connection that thrives.

NOTES

NOTES

NOTES

NOTES

CHAPTER 4

"Conflict is inevitable, but combat is optional."

– Max Lucado –

CHAPTER 4

Conflict. It's a four-letter word that can strike fear into the hearts of even the strongest couples. But here's the truth: conflict is inevitable. Disagreements happen – it's simply a part of any relationship. What truly matters is how you handle those disagreements.

Healthy conflict resolution is a cornerstone of a strong and lasting relationship. Here's why developing effective conflict resolution skills is essential for fostering deeper emotional connection:

Promotes Open Communication: Conflict resolution provides a platform to practice and refine communication skills. You learn to express your needs and feelings assertively, listen actively to your partner's perspective, and navigate difficult conversations with respect. This open and honest communication is the bedrock of any strong emotional connection.

Strengthens Your Bond: Working through conflict together is a form of teamwork. It demonstrates your commitment to the relationship and your willingness to invest time and effort to overcome challenges.Successfully resolving disagreements can create a sense of "us against the world" solidifying your bond and fostering a sense of security within the relationship.

CHAPTER 4

- **Enhances Empathy and Understanding:** Navigating conflict constructively allows you to see things from your partner's perspective. You gain a deeper understanding of their emotional triggers, values, and communication style. This newfound empathy strengthens your connection and fosters a sense of intimacy.

- **Provides Opportunities for Growth:** Conflict can be a catalyst for personal growth. By reflecting on your own behavior and reactions during disagreements, you can identify areas for improvement. Learning to manage your emotions effectively and communicate assertively benefits not only your relationship but also your overall well-being.

- **Builds Trust:** Successfully resolving conflict fosters trust within the relationship. Your partner sees that you're willing to be vulnerable, communicate openly, and work towards solutions together. This builds a foundation of trust and security, essential for emotional intimacy.

By developing these skills and approaching conflict with a collaborative mindset, you can navigate disagreements with greater ease. Remember, conflict resolution isn't about winning or placing blame.

CHAPTER 4

It's about nurturing emotional connection, building trust, and emerging from disagreements stronger and more connected than ever before.

THE STAGES OF CONFLICT

Conflict doesn't erupt out of nowhere. It often follows a predictable pattern:

- Stage 1: Build-Up: Underlying issues simmer beneath the surface. Frustrations and resentments build without being addressed.

- Stage 2: Trigger: A seemingly trivial event sparks the conflict, acting as a tipping point for the built-up tension.

- Stage 3: The Explosion: Emotions flare, and the argument erupts. Harsh words are exchanged, and blame is often placed.

- Stage 4: Withdrawal or Stonewalling: One or both partners shut down emotionally, withdrawing from communication.

CHAPTER 4

- **Stage 5: Repair or Distance:** The couple either attempts to repair the damage and rebuild trust, or the conflict festers, leading to emotional distance.

By understanding these stages, you can identify where you are in the conflict cycle and take steps to intervene before things escalate.

EFFECTIVE COMMUNICATION DURING CONFLICT

The way you communicate during conflict can significantly impact the outcome. Here are some key strategies for effective communication:

- **Active Listening:** This goes beyond simply hearing the words your partner says. Pay close attention to their nonverbal cues like body language and tone of voice. Show them you're engaged by making eye contact, nodding, and summarizing what you've heard.

- **"I" Statements:** Express how your partner's actions or words made you feel, rather than placing blame. For example, "I felt hurt when you said…" is more constructive than simply saying "You hurt me."

CHAPTER 4

- **Focus on the Issue:** Stay focused on the problem at hand, not bringing up past grievances or attacking your partner's character.

- **Validate Your Partner's Feelings:** Acknowledge their emotions, even if you don't necessarily agree. Phrases like "I understand why you feel that way" or "It sounds like you're feeling frustrated" can go a long way in de-escalating the situation.

- **Take Turns Talking:** Don't talk over each other. Give each other space to express yourselves without interruption.

By following these communication tips, you can create a safe space for open and honest conversation, even during heated moments.

MOVING FORWARD: REPAIRING THE DAMAGE

Even the healthiest couples fight sometimes. The important thing is to repair the damage and rebuild trust after an argument. Here are some steps to take:

CHAPTER 4

- **Allow Time to Cool Down:** Don't try to force a conversation if emotions are still running high. Give yourselves some space to calm down before attempting to talk things through.

- **Initiate the Conversation:** Once you've both calmed down, take the initiative to talk about the fight. Phrases like "I can see we're both upset. Can we talk about this when we've both calmed down?" or "I miss you. Can we give each other a hug?" can be a good starting point.

- **Take Responsibility:** Acknowledge your part in the argument and apologize sincerely if you said or did something hurtful. Owning your mistakes demonstrates respect and creates a foundation for rebuilding trust.

- **Practice Forgiveness:** Holding onto anger and resentment will only hinder the healing process. Forgive your partner for their part and focus on moving forward together. Forgiveness doesn't mean condoning their behavior, but rather letting go of negativity and choosing to rebuild the relationship

CHAPTER 4

- **Focus on Solutions:** Instead of dwelling on the past, work together to find solutions that address the underlying issues that led to the argument. What can you do differently next time to prevent a similar conflict?

- **Rebuild Trust:** Rebuilding trust takes time and effort. Consistent positive actions and open communication are key. Show your partner you're committed to the relationship through your actions, not just your words.

PHRASES TO INITIATE A CONVERSATION AFTER A FIGHT

Here are some additional phrases you can use to initiate a conversation after a fight:

- "I'm still feeling hurt by what you said earlier. Can we talk about it?"

- "I apologize for my part in the argument. How can we move forward?

- "I want to understand your perspective better. Can we talk about what happened?"

CHAPTER 4

- "I know we're both upset, but I value our relationship. Can we try to work through this together?"

The goal after a fight isn't to place blame or win an argument. It's about repairing the hurt, rebuilding trust, and moving forward in a healthy way.

Communication and vulnerability are opportunities for connection. Not talking about your feelings will cause resentment which will kill emotional intimacy.

Remember:

Conflict resolution is a skill that can be learned and improved over time.

By following the tips in this chapter and fostering open communication, you can navigate disagreements with greater ease and emerge from them with a stronger and more connected relationship.

NOTES

NOTES

NOTES

CHAPTER 5

"The willingness to resolve conflicts is the hallmark of a mature and healthy relationship."

– Unknown –

CHAPTER 5

Lasting connection isn't a guarantee, even in the most passionate relationships. Life throws curveballs, routines settle in, and sometimes those initial sparks can dim. The truth is, that both partners need to be willing to evolve and adapt.

Making time for emotional connection in your life often requires making intentional changes and prioritizing your relationship. What are some changes you need to make in your life to make more time for emotional connection?

Remember, a strong emotional connection is a garden that needs constant tending, but the effort you put in today blossoms into a lifetime of love and intimacy.

Here are some exercises to help you and your partner reconnect on a deeper level:

- **The 36 Questions Exercise:** This exercise, originally designed by psychologist Arthur Aron, involves asking each other 36 increasingly personal questions designed to foster intimacy and connection. You can find it here: https://shorturl.at/zZTc9

CHAPTER 5

- **The "Gratitude Jar"**: Keep a jar and throughout the week, write down small things you appreciate about your partner. During your check-in, take turns reading these notes aloud to each other. This simple exercise reinforces appreciation and strengthens the emotional bond.

- **Recreate Your First Date:** Plan an evening replicating your first date, or a special date that holds significance in your relationship. Reliving those early moments can spark nostalgia and remind you of the spark that drew you together. Talk about what attracted you to each other in the first place. Your first kiss, the first time you knew you loved each other.

- **The "Compliment Shower":** Set a timer for 2 minutes and take turns showering each other with compliments, focusing on both physical and personality traits. This exercise promotes positive

This challenge is designed to strengthen your emotional connection with your partner through small, daily acts of intentionality.

CHAPTER 5

7 DAYS OF EMOTIONAL CONNECTION

Day 1: Uninterrupted Attention

- Goal: Give your partner your undivided attention for a set period (15-30 minutes).
- Activity: Put away phones, turn off distractions, and simply listen to each other. This could be sharing about your day, a current challenge, or a dream.

Day 2: Appreciation Avalanche

- *Goal:* Shower your partner with compliments and appreciation.
- *Activity:* Throughout the day, verbally acknowledge something you appreciate about your partner, big or small. It could be a specific action, a personality trait, or simply their presence in your life.

Day 3: Shared Memories Lane

Goal: Rekindle positive memories and strengthen your bond.

CHAPTER 5

- *Activity:* Spend some time reminiscing about your relationship. Look through old photos, discuss your first date, or share a funny story from your past together.

Day 4: Love Language Adventure

- *Goal:* Learn and express love in ways your partner appreciates most.
- *Activity:* If you haven't yet, research the five love languages (words of affirmation, acts of service, receiving gifts, quality time, physical touch). Identify your partner's primary love language and plan a small act that speaks to it.

Day 5: Dream Team Brainstorm

- *Goal:* Reconnect on shared goals and aspirations.
- *Activity:* Spend time discussing your short-term and long-term goals. Talk about how you can support each other in achieving your dreams, both individually and as a couple.

CHAPTER 5

Day 6: The Power of Touch

- *Goal:* Increase physical intimacy and emotional connection.
- *Activity:* Engage in non-sexual touch throughout the day. This could be a hug, a handhold, a shoulder rub, or a back scratch. Physical touch releases oxytocin, a bonding hormone.

Day 7: Gratitude Reflection

- *Goal:* Express appreciation for your partner and the relationship.
- *Activity:* Write a heartfelt letter or note to your partner expressing your gratitude for their presence in your life. You can mention specific things you appreciate about them and your relationship.

CHAPTER 5

A JOURNEY, NOT A DESTINATION

Congratulations! You've reached the end of this exploration of emotional connection.

This journey of understanding yourself, your partner, and the dynamics of your relationship is a continuous one.

There will be moments of deep connection and laughter, and there will inevitably be times of misunderstanding and conflict.

Remember:

Emotional connection is not a fixed state; it's a journey of growth, vulnerability, and continuous effort.

By using the tools and strategies you've learned throughout this book, you can navigate the inevitable disconnects and emerge stronger together.

NOTES

NOTES

NOTES

FINAL THOUGHTS

Here are some final thoughts to carry with you:

- **Prioritize Connection**: Make emotional connection a priority in your relationship. Schedule regular check-ins, nurture intimacy, and be present in the moment. Be intentional about creating moments to connect.

- **Make time for fun**: Always have something to look forward to, even if it's a Friday morning coffee date.

- **Embrace Growth**: View challenges as opportunities for growth, both individually and as a couple.

- **Celebrate Milestones**: Take time to acknowledge and celebrate the moments of connection and intimacy you share.

The most important takeaway is this: a fulfilling emotional connection is within reach. By nurturing vulnerability, practicing effective communication, and fostering mutual respect, you can build a relationship that thrives and endures.

FROM THE AUTHOR

I hope this handbook has been as enlightening and helpful for you as it has been for me.

Remember, relationships are like gardens - they need nurturing, attention, and a little bit of sunshine to thrive.

So go ahead, water your love with empathy, understanding, and lots of laughter. And don't forget to give yourself and your partner a big ol' hug every now and then!

With Love,

Adele

Printed in Great Britain
by Amazon